SMART W[...] READ[...]

HURRICANES

Christine A. Caputo

SCHOLASTIC INC.
New York Toronto London Auckland
Sydney Mexico City New Delhi Hong Kong

What are SMART WORDS?

Smart Words are frequently used words that are critical to understanding concepts taught in the classroom. The more Smart Words a child knows, the more easily he or she will grasp important curriculum concepts. Smart Words Readers introduce these key words in a fun and motivational format while developing important literacy skills. Each new word is highlighted, defined in context, and reviewed. Engaging activities at the end of each chapter allow readers to practice the words they have learned.

ISBN 978-0-545-36824-7

Packaged by Q2AMedia

Copyright © 2011 by Scholastic Inc.

Picture Credit: t= top, b= bottom, l= left, r= right, c= center

Cover Page: Jim Edds/Science Photo Library/Photolibrary.
Title Page: Gail Johnson /Shutterstock.
Imprint Page: Jim Brooks/U.S. Navy.
Content Page: Jim Brooks/U.S. Navy.

4-5: Chris Hondros/Getty Images; 6-7: Skyphoto/Fotolia; 8-9: Jim Reed/Science Photo Library; 10: Image Science & Analysis Laboratory, NASA Johnson Space Center; 12: Nicholas Prior/Getty Images; 13: Zastol skiy Victor Leonidovich/Shutterstock; 14: Moorefam/iStockphoto; 16: Mario Tama/Getty Images; 19l: NASA; 19r: NOAA; 20: NOAA; 21t: Jocelyn Augustino/FEMA Photo Library; 21c: Zahner M.H./Stereograph Cards/ Library of Congress; 21b: NOAA; 23: Wilfredo Lee/AP Photo; 24-25: Bob Epstein/ FEMA Photo Library; 26: Gemphotography/Shutterstock; 28: Tracyhornbrook/Fotolia; 29: Jim Brooks/U.S. Navy.

Q2AMedia Art Bank: 7, 8, 11, 15, 18, 23, 25.

12 11 10 9 8 7 6   14 15 16/0

Printed in the U.S.A.   40
First printing, September 2011

Table of Contents

Chapter 1

A Violent Storm

The Outer Banks of North Carolina is a paradise of beaches, lighthouses, and wildlife. Herds of wild ponies call it home. However, paradise is sometimes interrupted. Like other areas along the eastern coast of the United States, the Outer Banks is often a target for hurricanes.

A **hurricane** is a strong, spinning weather system with winds that are faster than 74 miles (119 kilometers) per hour.

Every year hurricanes cause millions, even billions, of dollars in damage.

SMART WORD

hurricane a strong, spinning weather system with winds that are faster than 74 miles (119 kilometers) per hour

When a hurricane approaches, people gather to watch news of the storm. Orders may come for them to evacuate. Intense thunderstorms bringing raging winds and driving rains will soon be putting these people in danger.

But they know that the Outer Banks has survived many hurricanes over the years. Barrier islands along the coast break the harsh waves before they hit the mainland. Nature has a way of defending itself, ensuring that the Outer Banks will weather any storm.

The Winds of a Hurricane

The winds of a hurricane can pick a boat out of the water and toss it to shore like a toy. Yet a gentle summer breeze and a hurricane-force wind form in the same way.

Did you know that you have about one ton of force pushing on your body right now? That's about the same as having a 2,000-pound (907-kilogram) hippo on your back!

Air is made up of particles and has weight, just like everything else around you. The weight of air pushing down on Earth is called **air pressure**.

Greater differences in air pressure create stronger winds. Hurricane winds can be powerful enough to topple big ships at sea.

High pressure   Low pressure

Cold air   Warm air

Particles in cold air have little energy, so they don't move much and stay close together. Particles in warm air have more energy, so they move faster and farther apart.

All air does not have the same pressure. Fewer particles make warm air lighter than cool air, so it has lower air pressure. Cooler air has higher air pressure.

Warmer, lighter air rises. As it does, cooler air flows in to replace the rising air. This movement of air from areas of high pressure to areas of low pressure is called **wind**.

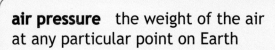

SMART WORDS

air pressure   the weight of the air at any particular point on Earth

wind   the flow of air from an area of high pressure to an area of low pressure

Feeding a Hurricane

Winds can turn into whirling monsters when they start to spin. A hurricane is actually a type of storm known as a **tropical cyclone**. This type of storm is made up of a system of thunderstorms that spin, or rotate, in a circle.

The clouds that spin in a tropical cyclone form above warm ocean waters. Warm, moist air over the ocean rises and cools, leaving an area of low air pressure near the surface.

The area of low pressure pulls nearby cool air into it. This air then becomes heated and rises, too.

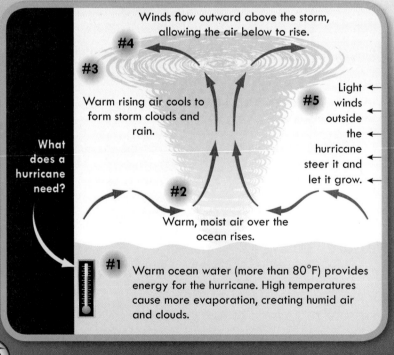

Winds flow outward above the storm, allowing the air below to rise.

#4

#3 Warm rising air cools to form storm clouds and rain.

#5 Light winds outside the hurricane steer it and let it grow.

What does a hurricane need?

#2 Warm, moist air over the ocean rises.

#1 Warm ocean water (more than 80°F) provides energy for the hurricane. High temperatures cause more evaporation, creating humid air and clouds.

When air rises, it cools to form storm clouds and rain. As air continues to rise and surrounding air swirls in to take its place, the spinning winds of the tropical cyclone grow.

In the Southern Hemisphere, tropical cyclones rotate in the same direction as the hands of clock turn, or clockwise. In the Northern Hemisphere, they rotate in the opposite direction, or counterclockwise. This is caused by the way Earth spins around on its axis.

SMART WORD

tropical cyclone a storm that has a low-pressure center surrounded by a spinning system of winds and rain

The Shape of a Hurricane

You would have no trouble recognizing a hurricane if you were in the middle of one — with trees bending in the wind and roofs blowing off. But, if you were an astronaut high above the Earth, you would get a very different view!

During one hurricane, astronauts on the International Space Station could see the Atlantic Ocean right through the **eye**, or center, of the hurricane. The eye is a region of relatively clear and calm conditions, about 20–40 miles (30–65 kilometers) wide.

This is a view from above the hurricane, as an astronaut orbiting Earth might see it!

eye

spiral band

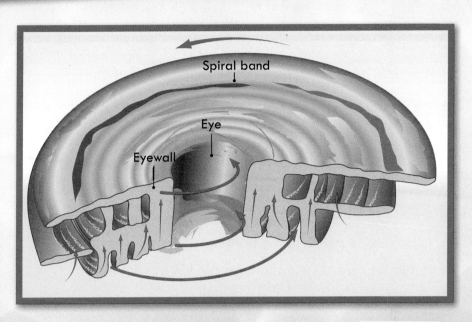

Spiral band

Eye

Eyewall

Immediately outside of the eye is the **eyewall** region. Conditions in the eyewall are opposite to those in the eye. This is the area with the strongest winds and the heaviest rains of the hurricane.

As a hurricane spins, regions of clouds produce intense conditions like those in the eyewall. One of these regions, known as a **spiral band**, may extend a few hundred miles outward from the center of the hurricane.

SMART WORDS

eye   the calm center of a swirling hurricane

eyewall   the region of intense wind and rain surrounding the eye of a hurricane

spiral band   the region of clouds that extend outward from the center of a hurricane, carrying strong winds and rain

Match each description with the correct Smart Word.

> hurricane   eye   eyewall   spiral band
> tropical cyclone   air pressure   wind

1. the calm center of a swirling hurricane

2. air that flows from an area of high pressure to an area of low pressure

3. the general name for a spinning system of wind and rain around an area of low pressure

4. the weight of air pushing down on Earth

5. the region of clouds that extend outward from the center of a hurricane, carrying strong winds and rain

6. an area of intense wind and rain just around the center of a hurricane

7. a strong, spinning weather system with winds that are faster than 74 miles (119 kilometers) per hour

Answers on page 32

Talk Like a Scientist

Imagine you are a weather reporter warning residents about an upcoming hurricane. Explain the conditions they will experience. Use your Smart Words in your description.

Did You Know?

Tropical cyclones always get started near the equator, where the sun's rays hit directly. They need warm ocean waters and light winds in order to form.

Is That a Fact?

In the North Atlantic, hurricane season is from June 1 to November 30. That's because the waters need to be warmed all summer for a hurricane to form.

Did You Know?

If a tropical cyclone forms in the western North Pacific Ocean, it is called a typhoon. If it forms in the North Atlantic Ocean, South Pacific Ocean, or Northeast Pacific Ocean, it is called a hurricane.

Chapter 2

The Path of DESTRUCTION

Once formed, a hurricane begins to travel. The spinning winds are pushed along by other winds high in the air above Earth. As the hurricane moves toward land, it can turn deadly even before hitting the coast.

As the hurricane's winds spiral around and around, they push water into a mound at the storm's center. The mound of water, called a **storm surge**, gets pushed forward onto land. Although it varies, a storm surge can be 18 feet (5.5 meters) tall!

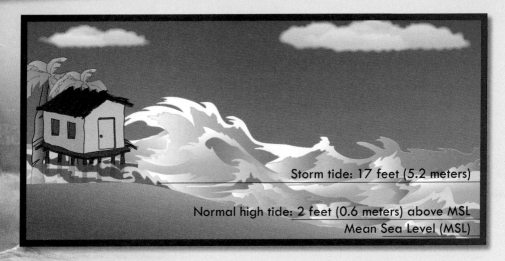

Storm tide: 17 feet (5.2 meters)

Normal high tide: 2 feet (0.6 meters) above MSL
Mean Sea Level (MSL)

If a storm surge occurs at the same time as a high tide, the combination is called a **storm tide**. During a storm tide, the water level rises well above normal. Such a tremendous amount of water quickly pouring onto land may cause disastrous **flooding**.

Some of the water that reaches land causes **erosion**. During erosion, particles of rock, sand, and soil are carried away. This can wear away coastlines, leaving them open to more flooding.

SMART WORDS

storm surge   a mound of water formed by winds that is pushed onto land

storm tide   a storm surge that occurs at the same time as high tide

flooding   an overflow of water onto a region of land

erosion   the process through which water and other forces carry away particles of rock, sand, and soil

Measuring Hurricanes

As a hurricane forms out in the ocean, scientists begin to keep an eye on it. Hurricanes can gain or lose strength depending on the availability of the warm water that fuels them.

Perhaps you have heard a hurricane described as a Category 1 or Category 4. These numbers come from the **Saffir–Simpson Hurricane Wind Scale**. The ratings on this scale span from 1 to 5. The weakest hurricane has a rating of 1 and the strongest storm is rated 5. The Saffir–Simpson scale uses two categories to describe a hurricane.

With several large trees down, this damage may have been caused by a Category 3 hurricane.

The first category is the speed of the wind. Hurricane winds can range from 74 miles (119 kilometers) per hour to more than 155 miles (249 kilometers) per hour. Sometimes the winds get spinning so fast that a storm known as a **tornado** forms.

The second category is the damage the storm does. While a weaker storm might produce minimal damage, a strong storm can be catastrophic.

Saffir–Simpson Hurricane Wind Scale		
Category	Winds (MPH)	Damage
1	74–95	**Very Dangerous:** Large tree branches will snap, damage to power lines will cause outages, damage may occur to older framed homes and older or unanchored mobile homes.
2	96–110	**Extremely Dangerous:** Many trees with shallow roots will be uprooted, near total power loss may last for several days to weeks, damage may occur to roof structures of poorly constructed homes, and older mobile homes have a high chance of being destroyed.
3	111–130	**Devastating:** Roads will be blocked as many trees are uprooted, electricity and water will be unavailable for several days to a few weeks, nearly all older mobile homes will be destroyed, newer mobile homes and frame houses will sustain severe damage.
4	131–155	**Catastrophic:** Many roads will be blocked as most trees are snapped or uprooted, power outages and long-term water shortages will occur, most of the area will be uninhabitable for weeks or months, many poorly constructed frame homes and nearly all older mobile homes will be destroyed.
5	More than 155	**Catastrophic:** Nearly all trees will be snapped or uprooted, electricity and water will be unavailable for weeks to possibly months, the areas will be uninhabitable for weeks or months, a high percentage of frame homes and almost all mobile homes will be destroyed.

SMART WORDS

Saffir–Simpson Hurricane Wind Scale a measurement system used to rate hurricanes according to their intensity

tornado a violent storm made up of spinning column of air

Tracking Hurricanes

Hurricane Katrina, one of the most devastating storms in U.S. history, started in the warm waters around the Bahamas. Weather forecasters identified the storm and followed its path, or **track**, as it traveled toward Florida. This gave people living there time to prepare.

Scientists also monitor hurricanes using **weather satellites**. A satellite orbits around Earth in space. The satellite gathers information about winds, temperature, and other conditions and sends it to computers on the ground.

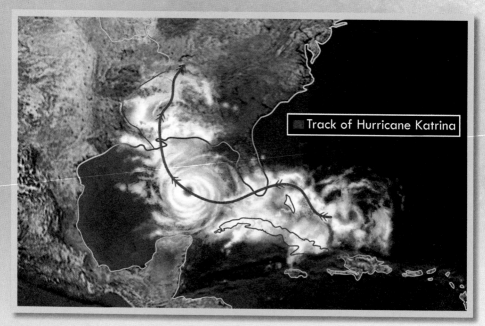

Track of Hurricane Katrina

Using information from weather satellites and storm models, scientists tracked the path of Hurricane Katrina.

Weather satellites orbiting Earth send pictures of storms to computers on the ground.

Scientists use the information from satellites to form a "picture," or **model** of the storm. A storm model shows details about the storm, such as where it is likely to go.

Across the country, people watched on their televisions as Hurricane Katrina traveled from Florida over the warm waters of the Gulf of Mexico. As it became a Category 5 hurricane, people living in Louisiana and Mississippi prepared for the storm.

SMART WORDS

track the path a storm, such as a hurricane, might take

weather satellite a device that orbits Earth collecting information about weather conditions

model an image of a storm based on data collected by satellites, airplanes, and other methods

Use your SMART WORDS

Read each clue. Choose the Smart Word it describes.

> **weather satellite**   **storm tide**   **storm surge**
>
> **tornado**   **flooding**   **erosion**   **model**
>
> **track**   **Saffir–Simpson Hurricane Wind Scale**

1. I am the path that a hurricane takes.

2. I am a measurement system used to rate the intensity of a hurricane.

3. I am what happens when water covers land.

4. I am a storm surge that happens during high tide.

5. I am a mound of water that is pushed onto land during a hurricane.

6. I am the process of carrying bits of rock, sand, and soil to new places.

7. I am a picture of a storm made by data collected in space and on Earth.

8. I am a storm made up of a spinning column of air.

9. I am a device that orbits Earth collecting information about weather conditions.

Answers on page 32

Talk Like a Scientist

Explain how scientists use data from satellites to track hurricanes. Use your Smart Words in your explanation.

20

Costliest Hurricane

Hurricane Katrina in 2005 is considered the costliest hurricane ever in terms of damage. The hurricane left New Orleans with over $75 billion in damages.

Most Deadly Hurricane

In 1900, a major hurricane hit along the coast of Galveston, Texas. Modern methods of tracking storms were not available. More than 6,000 people lost their lives.

Fastest Winds

Hurricane Camille in 1969 began as a small storm in the Caribbean. It developed into a hurricane with winds so fast they destroyed the equipment set up to measure their speed on the Mississippi coast.

Landfall!

The day before Katrina made landfall, satellite images showed it was headed for the Louisiana–Mississippi border.

People known as **hurricane hunters** flew directly into the storm. They took measurements of the air pressure inside the hurricane.

Based on information from weather forecasters, people had already been ordered to evacuate the area. During an **evacuation**, people must leave their homes and move to a safer area.

For those who stay behind when a hurricane hits land, the events can be remarkable. The sky darkens as clouds from the spiral band begin to appear. As the storm advances, winds howl around buildings and rain begins to pour down. The storm has made landfall.

hurricane hunter a person who travels into a hurricane to gather information about it

evacuation the process in which people leave an area to move to safer locations

Look Out

Once a hurricane hits land, it no longer has warm water to feed it, and it quickly dies. In its wake, there is often a path of destruction — damaged buildings, flooding, and erosion.

Predicting exactly where a hurricane will make landfall is no easy task. As scientists work to narrow down the possible paths of a storm, they issue advisories to people living where the hurricane might go.

Regions that are issued a **hurricane watch** may experience the conditions of a hurricane. People are advised to prepare by gathering the supplies they need, staying indoors, and paying attention to weather reports. A hurricane watch is usually issued up to 48 hours before the strong winds are expected.

Hurricane watches and warnings can't prevent all damage, but they can help people prepare for the storm and stay safe.

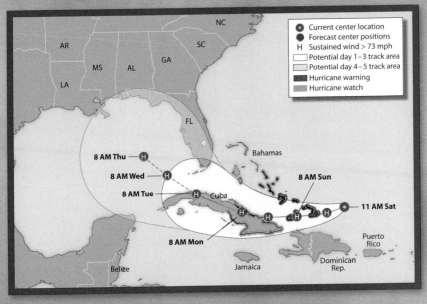

Legend:
- ● Current center location
- ● Forecast center positions
- H Sustained wind > 73 mph
- ☐ Potential day 1–3 track area
- ☐ Potential day 4–5 track area
- ■ Hurricane warning
- ■ Hurricane watch

Map labels: NC, SC, AR, GA, MS, AL, LA, FL, Bahamas, Cuba, Jamaica, Belize, Dominican Rep., Puerto Rico

8 AM Thu, 8 AM Wed, 8 AM Tue, 8 AM Mon, 8 AM Sun, 11 AM Sat

Maps are used to track the path of the hurricane and show areas where advisories have been issued.

If a **hurricane warning** is issued, hurricane conditions are expected within 36 hours. Once the conditions arrive, it is too late to prepare. People are urged to get ready before the warning is issued.

SMART WORDS

hurricane watch an advisory for coastal regions issued when hurricane conditions are possible within 48 hours

hurricane warning an advisory for coastal regions issued when hurricane conditions are expected within 36 hours

EVACUATION
UNDERWAY

Protecting Lives and Homes

One of the most important things anyone
can do to prepare for a hurricane is to have a plan
long before the first hurricane watch is issued.
People who live in areas that are frequently hit by
hurricanes know to listen to weather forecasts.

They know to have supplies in place to protect themselves, their homes, and even their pets! When orders are given to evacuate the area, it is important to know where to go, what to bring, and how to get there. Sometimes people wait out a hurricane or are unable to evacuate. Under these circumstances, people must pay attention to flooding conditions.

When flooding occurs, sewers can overflow, dumping contaminated materials into the drinking water supply. This is why it is important to keep bottled water in a hurricane supply kit.

Other items in a hurricane supply kit might include a battery-operated radio, flashlight, extra batteries, canned foods and a manual can opener, and a first-aid kit.

Hurricane Supply Kit

- ☑ First-aid supplies and prescription medications for 2 weeks
- ☑ Canned food supplies for 3–5 days and a manual can opener
- ☑ Minimum of 3 gallons of drinking water per person
- ☑ Protective clothing, rainwear, bedding or sleeping bags
- ☑ Battery-powered radio, flashlight, clock
- ☑ Batteries
- ☑ Full gas tank
- ☑ Fully charged cell phone with a car charger accessory

Answer each question with a Smart Word.

| hurricane hunter | hurricane watch |
| hurricane warning | evacuation |

1. Which type of advisory is issued when hurricane conditions might occur within 48 hours?

2. Through which process do people travel to safer locations?

3. Which type of advisory is issued when hurricane conditions are expected right away?

4. What name describes a person who travels into a hurricane to gather information about it?

Answers on page 32

Talk Like a Scientist

Write out a hurricane plan that a family living along a coastline might use. Use your Smart Words to describe how they should prepare for a possible hurricane.

SMART FACTS

Did You Know?

Once the winds from a tropical cyclone reach 39 miles (62.8 kilometers) per hour, the storm is given a name.

Record Storms

If a storm is particularly devastating, its name is retired and never used again to describe a tropical cyclone. *Katrina* was retired in 2005 and *Andrew* in 1992.

That's Interesting

In 1979, the National Hurricane Center selected six lists of names to be used in different years to name hurricanes. The names go back and forth between girl names and boy names.

Glossary

air pressure the weight of the air at any particular point on Earth

erosion the process through which water and other forces carry away particles of rock, sand, and soil

evacuation the process in which people leave an area to move to safer locations

eye the calm center of a swirling hurricane

eyewall the region of intense wind and rain surrounding the eye of a hurricane

flooding an overflow of water onto a region of land

hurricane a strong, spinning weather system with winds that are faster than 74 miles (119 kilometers) per hour

hurricane hunter a person who travels into a hurricane to gather information about it

hurricane warning an advisory for coastal regions issued when hurricane conditions are expected within 36 hours

hurricane watch an advisory for coastal regions issued when hurricane conditions are possible within 48 hours

model an image of a storm based on data collected by satellites, airplanes, and other methods

Saffir–Simpson Hurricane Wind Scale a measurement system used to rate hurricanes according to their intensity

spiral band the region of clouds that extend outward from the center of a hurricane, carrying strong winds and rain

storm surge a mound of water formed by winds that is pushed onto land

storm tide a storm surge that occurs at the same time as high tide

tornado a violent storm made up of a spinning column of air

track the path a storm, such as a hurricane, might take

tropical cyclone a storm that has a low-pressure center surrounded by a spinning system of winds and rain

weather satellite a device that orbits Earth collecting information about weather conditions

wind the flow of air from an area of high pressure to an area of low pressure

Index

SMART WORDS Answer Key

Page 12
1. eye, 2. wind, 3. tropical cyclone, 4. air pressure,
5. spiral band, 6. eyewall, 7. hurricane

Page 20
1. track, 2. Saffir–Simpson Hurricane Wind Scale, 3. flooding,
4. storm tide, 5. storm surge, 6. erosion, 7. model, 8. tornado,
9. weather satellite

Page 28
1. hurricane watch, 2. evacuation, 3. hurricane warning,
4. hurricane hunter

SMART WORDS
READER
HURRICANES

Destructive hurricanes make the news every year. These giant storms travel across oceans, building in strength, until they hit land. When hurricanes do make landfall—WATCH OUT!—their powerful winds, pounding rain, and massive flooding can destroy homes, towns, even big cities. Hunt for information about hurricanes in this book and build your science Smart Word vocabulary!

■ SCHOLASTIC
www.scholastic.com

ISBN 978-0-545-36824-

EAN

9 780545 368247

08-BAC-575

FROM THE AUTHOR OF *HAPPY TOGETHER*

JOHN BOSIO

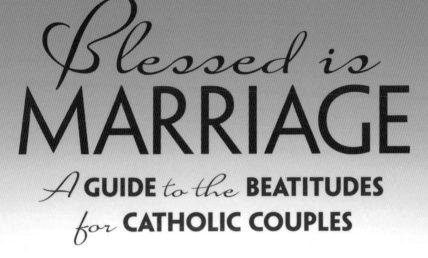

Blessed is

MARRIAGE

A GUIDE *to the* BEATITUDES
for CATHOLIC COUPLES

"This deeply insightful
and practical book outlines
simple ways to take your
marriage to the next level."

MATTHEW KELLY
AUTHOR AND FOUNDER OF *DYNAMICCATHOLIC.COM*